ENCOURAGEMENT

40 DAYS OF

ENCOURAGEMENT

In-depth personal reflections to guide you to discover God's words of encouragement that you may find the strength to persevere.

Rita Kroon

Seek the Lord to fill your empty cup with your daily portion that you may be filled with encouragement.

A Walk to the Well

The author has represented and warranted full ownership and/or legal right to publish all the materials in this book.

40 Days Encouragement All Rights Reserved.
Copyright © 2015 2018 2023 Rita Kroon

Cover Photo © Thinkstock. All rights reserved – used with permission.

A Walk to the Well
www.awalktothewell.com

This book may not be reproduced, transmitted, or stored in whole or in part by any means, including graphics, electronic, or mechanical without the express written consent of the publisher except in the case of brief quotation embodied in critical articles and reviews.

ISBN: 978-0-9891985-4-7

A Walk to the Well and its logo are trademarks belonging to A Walk to the Well.

Unless otherwise indicated, all Scripture quotations are from the Holy Bible, New American Standard Bible. Copyright Lockman Foundation, 1960, 1962, 1963, 1968, 1971, 1972, 1973, 1975, 1984 by International Bible Society. Used with permission. Scripture quotations identified ESV are from the Holy Bible English Standard Version. Copyright 2001 by Crossway Bibles. Used with permission.
All rights reserved.

Printed on acid-free paper in the United States of America

Dedication

My current works are written in loving memory of
my husband, Burt, and our daughter, Rene',
my other two daughters, LaDawn and Shelly,
their husbands, my sister, Gayle
and my grandchildren all whom
I love and cherish
and for all who have ever been
encouraged by the Promises of God.

Rita Kroon

TABLE OF CONTENTS

DAY 1 ~ LIFE AND PEACE 1
DAY 2 ~ ETERNAL LIFE 3
DAY 3 ~ DRAW NEAR TO GOD 5
DAY 4 ~ RAISED UP ON THE LAST DAY 7
DAY 5 ~ SECURE IN GOD'S HANDS 9
DAY 6 ~ ESCAPE JUDGMENT 11
DAY 7 ~ DOERS OF THE WORD 13
DAY 8 ~ ABIDE IN CHRIST 15
DAY 9 ~ CROWN OF LIFE 17
DAY 10 ~ ETERNAL LIFE 19
DAY 11 ~ ALL NEEDS SUPPLIED 21
DAY 12 ~ ENTRANCE INTO KINGDOM 23
DAY 13 ~ TO BE BLESSED 25
DAY 14 ~ BELIEF IN GOD'S FAITHFULNESS 27
DAY 15 ~ BE FOUND BLAMELESS 29
DAY 16 ~ PROMISE FOR A FUTURE 31
DAY 17 ~ PEACE OF MIND 33
DAY 18 ~ ANSWERED PRAYER 35
DAY 19 ~ TRANSGRESSIONS WIPED OUT 37
DAY 20 ~ LET LOVE BE GENUINE 39
DAY 21 ~ ASSURANCE THAT GOD IS GOD 41
DAY 22 ~ WAIT WITH EAGER EXPECTATION .. 43
DAY 23 ~ FULLNESS OF JOY & PLEASURES 45
DAY 24 ~ TRUE WISDOM 47
DAY 25 ~ ASSURANCE OF ETERNAL LIFE 49
DAY 26 ~ CLEAR CONSCIENCE 51
DAY 27 ~ RENEWAL 53
DAY 28 ~ WAIT FOR THE LORD 55
DAY 29 ~ DELIVERANCE FROM DARKNESS 57

DAY 30 ~ LIVE IN THE MOMENT	59
DAY 31 ~ ABUNDANT LIFE	61
DAY 32 ~ SPIRIT-FILLED	63
DAY 33 ~ HOPE IN GOD	65
DAY 34 ~ QUIET AND GENTLE SPIRIT	67
DAY 35 ~ SECURITY	69
DAY 36 ~ STRENGTHENED WITH POWER	71
DAY 37 ~ PEACE WITH GOD	73
DAY 38 ~ EXULT IN THE LORD	75
DAY 39 ~ LET US BE THANKFUL	77
DAY 40 ~ REST FOR THE SOUL	79
MEET THE AUTHOR	84
OTHER BOOKS BY RITA KROON	86

Introduction

May this be your expectation every morning as you  bring your empty cup before the Lord: that He would fill your cup with your **daily portion** from His Word that you may drink deeply and be nourished. *Lord, You have assigned me my portion and my cup. You have made my lot secure. Psalm 16:5*

Each day has a key verse for the topic at hand set within the context of the preceding and following verses. The **goal** of the passage of Scripture along with **obstacles** that may stand in the way of attaining the goal, **affirmations** that reinforce the truth of God's Word, and a **personal application to apply to your own life**. Two personal questions follow that you <u>ask yourself</u> to prayerfully examine your heart to determine if you are reaching your goal and what may be hindering you.

Do you feel like you want to give up? Bombarded with negative thoughts? Disheartened over bad choices? Feeling down about your lot in life, perhaps? Lost all hope? Despairing over broken relationships? Seeing the future through the bleakness of the past? Look up. This collection of forty daily devotionals will help you see that God is a reservoir of strength. He has what is needed so that you may be able to persevere in trials. He has plans to give you a future and a hope.

God made promises to each of us in His written Word. God promised: faith for every challenge, forgiveness for every confessed sin, truth to counter every lie, success in every endeavor as God measures success, aid in every battle, help in every failure, wisdom for every decision, peace for every circumstance, strength for every task He calls us to do, supply for every lack, comfort in every trial, hope for every crisis, guidance for every dilemma, and security in every storm. Believers are encouraged by God's faithfulness because God cannot lie.

Bring your empty cup to the Lord that He may fill it with your daily portion of His grace to sustain you in time of need.

Come, drink deeply of God's word and be encouraged. Fill your cup and be satisfied in the Lord Jesus Christ.

Day 1 ~ Life and Peace

Read Romans 7:21-8:2

Romans 8:1 *"There is therefore now no condemnation for those who are in Christ Jesus."*

Goal: To obtain life and peace

Obstacles: Inability of the flesh to keep the law, war between the flesh and the mind, not understanding how to have victory, presence of evil, and the law of sin.

Affirmations: Paul writes to the Romans that Jesus Christ our Lord has set us free from the law of sin and death, that God sent His Son in the likeness of sinful man, yet without sin, as an offering for sin, and that Jesus fulfilled the requirement of the law which is death because of sin.

Personal Application of the Principle: Believers have been set free from the law of sin and death.

Result: We have life and peace with God, Jesus is glorified, and there is no condemnation for those of us who are in Christ Jesus.

Ask yourself
How do I receive life and peace with God?

Why can the Law not give peace, and how does grace apply to this question? (See Ephesians 2: 8-9 for additional clarification)

Day 2 ~ Eternal Life

Read John 3:25-36

John 3:36 *"Whoever believes in the Son has eternal life, whoever does not obey the Son shall not see life, but the wrath of God remains on him."*
(ESV)

Goal: To have eternal life and joy

Obstacles: Unbelief and disobedience

Affirmations: John bore witness to Christ Jesus as the bridegroom and to know Him is to know His joy completely. Jesus is from heaven and bears witness of heaven. He speaks of what He has seen and heard, He gives the Spirit without measure, and t the Father has given all things into His hand.

Personal Application of the Precepts: Since Jesus has borne witness of heaven and has revealed that to us, we desire to believe in Him and to be obedient to Him. We want to witness of Him. We decrease in presence that He may increase, and we acknowledge that we can do nothing apart from Him.

Result: We believe in Jesus Christ, we have eternal life, and our joy is made complete.

Ask yourself: How did I come to believe in Jesus Christ for eternal life?

How am I encouraged by knowing that because of God's grace, His wrath is averted from me give?

Day 3 ~ Draw Near to God

Read James 4:1-10

James 4:7-8 *"Submit yourselves therefore to God. Resist the devil and he will flee from you. Draw near to God and He will draw near to you."* (ESV)

Goal: To draw near to God

Obstacles: Conflicts and quarrels, lust, murder, envy, wrong motives, selfishness, spiritual adultery, friendship with the world, pride, the devil, and turmoil within self

Affirmations: James states that the Holy Spirit indwells us and longs jealously over us. God's grace is greater than our sin, He gives grace to the humble and will exalt the humble, and if we resist the devil, he will flee,

Personal Application of the Precepts: Inner conflict is caused by trying to have dual friendships – with the world and with God. We cannot lust for pleasures or to be greedy for things, so if we ask with wrong motives, we will not receive what we ask for. We are to be faithful. We can be confident that the Spirit longs jealously over us for our good.

We desire to be friends with God more so than with the world. We receive God's grace if we humble ourselves. When we draw near to God, He strengthens us, to resist the devil who will flee from us when we resist him.

Result: We draw near to God.

Ask yourself: What is a benefit of drawing near to God?

How do I resist the devil, and when I do, what happens?

Day 4 ~ Raised up on the Last Day

Read John 6:27-40

John 6:40 *"For this is the will of My Father, that everyone who beholds the Son and believes in Him, may have eternal life, and I myself will raise him up on the last day."*

Goal: To be raised up on the last day

Obstacles: Unbelief, works for earthly life, trusting in ancestors for salvation, seeking only temporary food, and hardness of heart

Affirmations: In his letter, John writes that there is food which endures to eternal life, that the Father has set His seal on Jesus, and the work of God is that we believe in Jesus. The Father (not Moses) gave manna in the wilderness, the Father gives the true bread out of heaven, and the True Bread gives life to the world. Jesus is the True Bread and whoever believes in Him shall never hunger or thirst. All the Father gives to Jesus shall come to Him and He will not cast us out. This is the will of God - all who believe in Jesus will have eternal life, and Jesus Himself will raise us up on the last day.

Personal Application of the Precepts: We will focus on things that count for eternity. We know Jesus and believe He is the true Bread from heaven. We are eager to do the *work of God* namely, to believe in Jesus since we know the *will of God* is that we believe in His Son. We come to Jesus and shall be satisfied. Therefore, the work of God and the will of God for us is to believe in Jesus.

Result: We have eternal life, and Jesus will raise us up on the last day to be with Him forever.

Ask yourself: How does the promise "all who believe in Jesus will have eternal life" give you peace?

What earthly things occupy my thoughts and distract me from thinking on things of eternity?

Day 5 ~ Secure in God's Hands

Read John 10:24-30

John 10:28-29 "*...and I give them eternal life, and they shall never perish, and no one shall snatch them out of My hand. My Father, who has given them to Me, is greater than all, and no one is able to snatch them out of the Father's hand.*" (ESV)

Goal: To know the security of being in God's hands

Obstacles: Hearing, but not believing

Affirmations: John says that the works done by Jesus in the Father's name bear witness that He is the Christ, and those who believe are counted as Jesus' sheep. Believers hear His voice, Jesus knows His own, believers follow Jesus, He gives believers eternal life, and no one is able to snatch them out of His hand. All who are saved have been given to Jesus by the Father. Jesus and His Father are perfect in unity in their natures and their actions.

Personal Application of the Precepts: As our hearts are opened to the truth, we believe that Jesus is the Christ and as believers, we are counted among the sheep of Jesus. Like sheep who hear the shepherd's voice, likewise we hear His voice and follow Him. Jesus knows us, and we can have confidence and assurance that He gives us eternal life, and no one can snatch us away.

Result: We are secure in God's hands.

<u>Ask yourself:</u> Who do I need to encourage, and to pray for, that they may have the security of eternal life?

Where do I need encouragement?

Day 6 ~ Escape Judgment

Read John 3:16-21

John 3:18 *"He who believes in Him is not judged, he who does not believe in Him has been judged already because he has not believed in the name of the only begotten Son of God."*

Goal: To escape judgment

Obstacles: Love of darkness, unbelief, evil deeds, hater of God, and pride

Affirmations: John states that Jesus did not come into the world to judge the world, but in order that the world might be saved through Him, and whoever believes is not judged. Jesus is the ONLY begotten Son of God; He is the light of the world that exposes the evil of those who love the darkness. Those who practice the truth come to the light that their deeds may be manifested as having been wrought in God.

Personal Application of the Precepts: Jesus is the light, and if we practice the truth, we will have fellowship with Him on earth and will receive eternal life. We believe that Jesus is the only begotten Son of God and that He is the Savior of the world to those who believe. Our deeds will be shown as having been wrought in God.

Result: We escape judgment.

<u>Ask yourself</u>: Why would I be counted among those who believe in Jesus and do not come into judgment?

How did I come to believe that Jesus is the Light of the world?

Day 7 ~ Doers of the Word

Read James 1:19-27

James 1:22-24 *"But be doers of the word and not hearers only deceiving yourselves. For if anyone is a hearer of the word and not a doer, he is like the man who looks intently at his natural face in the mirror. He looks at himself and goes away and at once forgets what he was like."* (ESV)

Goal: To become doers of the word and not hearers only.

Obstacles: Filthiness and wickedness, pride, being deceived, ignoring the written word which is the ethical guide for Christian living and the standard for judgment, anger, religious deception

Affirmations: James writes that in humility, we are to receive the word into our hearts which is able to save our souls. We study the perfect law (law of liberty) and abide by it so that we shall be blessed in what we do. it is good for us to practice righteousness and not vain religion, to visit orphans and widows in distress, and to keep oneself unstained by the world which is pleasing to God.

Personal Application of the Precepts: If we receive the written word of God into our hearts, study the perfect law and abide by it, we will be blessed in what we do. As we strive to practice righteousness, and not vain religion, by keeping ourselves unstained by the world, we will please God.

Result: We will purpose to be doers of the word and not hearers only.

Ask yourself: If others were to observe me, would they say, "She is a doer of the word?" In other words, "She walks the talk." Why?

What must I do to practice righteousness and not vain religion? What is the difference?

Day 8 ~ Abide in Christ

Read John 15:1-11

John 15:7 *"If you abide in Me, and My words abide in you, ask whatever you wish, and it will be done for you."*

Goal: To abide in Christ and produce fruit

Obstacles: Disobedience, rebellion, hypocrisy

Affirmations: John states that **if** you surrender to Jesus and abide in Him, you can ask for whatever you wish, and it will be done for you. If you abide in Jesus, you will produce fruit. The Father is glorified through answered prayer, and prayer is answered if you abide in Jesus and His words abide you.

Personal Application of the Precepts: If we abide in Jesus and His words abide in us, we can ask for whatever we wish, and it will be done because we will be praying according to Jesus' commands and the Father's will. We will not ask amiss since we will be praying with the mind of Christ. If we abide in Jesus, we will keep his commandment to love one another, the Father will be glorified, we will produce fruit and have abundant joy. This cycle is repeated throughout our journey of faith and grows us spiritually.

Result: We will abide in Christ and will produce much fruit.

<u>Ask yourself:</u> What does it mean to 'abide in Jesus?'

What is meant by 'fruit?'

Day 9 ~ Crown of Life

Read James 1:2-12

James 1:12 *"Blessed is a man who perseveres under trial, for once he has been approved, he will receive the crown of life, which the Lord has promised to those who love Him."*

Goal: To receive the crown of life

Obstacles: Doubt, double-mindedness, instability, pride, pursuit of riches

Affirmations: James writes that believers should consider it joy to encounter trials. Why? Because the testing of faith produces endurance, and to let endurance have its perfect result – the testing of one's faith is designed to perfect one, so he is lacking nothing. God gives wisdom without reproach to those who ask in faith, and blessed is the one who perseveres under trial with approval from God.

Personal Application of the Precepts: We are encouraged to encounter trials with joy knowing that the testing of our faith produces endurance which results in our completeness – lacking in nothing. We are assured that if we ask God for wisdom, He will give it to us without reproach. Our faith is undivided, and we will receive God's reward, which is the crown of life.

Result: We will receive the crown of life which the Lord has promised to those who love Him.

<u>Ask yourself</u>: How can I be confident that I will receive the crown of life?

How do I respond to trials in my life, and how does Revelation 2:10 encourage me?

Day 10 ~ Eternal Life

Read 1 John 2:21-26

1 John 2:25 *"And this is the promise which He Himself made to us: eternal life."*

Goal: To receive eternal life

Obstacles: Not knowing the truth of God's Word, lying, denial that Jesus is the Christ (antichrist), denial of the Father and the Son, being deceived

Affirmations: In his letter, John writes that we know the truth, and the one who confesses the Son has the Father. We are to let the word of truth abide in us and if we do, we will abide in the Son and in the Father. This is the promise God Himself made to us while worldly people are trying to deceive us.

Personal Application of the Precepts: Since we know the truth of God, we can confidently confess the Son, and we can be assured that if we abide in the Son, we also abide in the Father. We can be encouraged to know and to trust in God's promise of eternal life.

Result: We will obtain eternal life.

Ask yourself: How can I tell an unbelieving friend the importance of believing the truth of God's Word?

In what ways do I confess the Son with confidence?

Day 11 ~ All Needs Supplied

Read Philippians 4:10-19

Phil. 4:19 *"And my God shall supply all your needs according to His riches in glory in Christ Jesus."* (ESV)

Goal: To have all our needs supplied

Obstacles: Withholding from those in need, and selfishness

Affirmations: In his letter to the Philippians, Paul writes that in any and every circumstance, he has learned the secret of having plenty and being in need – the secret being that we can do all things through Jesus Christ who strengthens us. The church of Philippi shared in the ministry of Paul, and he commended them for doing so. The gift itself is not what Paul sought, but rather that the profit would be added to their account since giving as a church toward missionaries is a fragrant aroma, an acceptable sacrifice, and well-pleasing to God. God will supply all the needs of the churches that give to missionaries.

Personal Application of the Precepts: As believing members of the local church, and as individuals in the body of Christ, we can know the secret of being content with what we have. The secret is that we can do all things through Christ Jesus. We know too, that when a church gives to missionaries for the furthering of the Gospel, the church will have its own needs supplied. Giving towards meeting the needs of others is a fragrant aroma, an acceptable sacrifice, and is well-pleasing to God.

Result: When we give to the needs of others, all our needs will be supplied according to the riches in glory in Jesus.

Ask yourself: How do I show my trust in God that He will supply all my needs when I contribute to the needs of others?

If I can only afford to give a meager contribution, will my offering still be a sweet aroma to God? How can I know for sure?

Day 12 ~ Entrance into Kingdom

Read 2 Peter 1:1-11

2 Peter 1:11 *"...for in this way the entrance into the eternal kingdom of our Lord and Savior will be abundantly supplied to you."*

Goal: To have entrance into the eternal kingdom

Obstacles: Corruption, lust, unbelief, ungodliness, unfruitfulness, spiritually blind, sin

Affirmations: Peter claims that Jesus' divine power has granted everything pertaining to life and godliness through the true knowledge of God who called you by His own glory and excellence. He granted to you His precious and magnificent promises so that you might become partakers of the divine nature. Diligence in faith brings moral excellence, knowledge, self-control, perseverance, godliness, brotherly kindness, love, and if these qualities are in you and increasing, then you are neither useless or unfruitful in the true knowledge of Jesus Christ. If we are diligent about His calling and choosing, and if we practice these things, we will not stumble.

Personal Application of the Precepts: Everything pertaining to life and godliness has been granted to us by God's divine power through the true knowledge of Him. He called us by His own glory and excellence and He granted to us His precious and magnificent promises that we might share in the life of God through Christ and the indwelling Holy Spirit. If we are diligent to practice pursuing godly qualities, we are useful and fruitful in the true knowledge of Jesus Christ and we will not stumble.

Result: The entrance into the eternal kingdom of our Lord and Savior Jesus Christ will be abundantly supplied to us.

Ask yourself: How do I pursue being diligent in pursuing godly qualities?

Why is it important for me to practice godly qualities?

Day 13 ~To Be Blessed

Read Act 3:13-26

Acts 3:25 *"It is you who are the sons of the prophets and of the covenant which God made with your fathers saying to Abraham, 'And in your seed all the families of the earth shall be blessed.'"*

Goal: To be blessed

Obstacles: Unbelief, ignorance, sin, and unrepentance, and the ignoring of Jesus.

Affirmations: Luke writes that Jesus is the seed of Abraham in whom all the families of the earth shall be blessed. He is the Holy and Righteous One, the Prince of life, that was put to death, but God raised Him from the dead. The crippled man was healed based on faith in the name of Jesus. God announced beforehand that His Christ should suffer and die for all sins, and the repentance of sins brings forgiveness, and times of refreshing that come from the presence of the Lord Jesus Christ who was appointed for you. Jesus is in heaven until the period of restoration of sinners is complete as foretold by the prophets of old. God frees you from your sins.

Personal Application of the Precepts: We have faith that Jesus is the seed of Abraham, the Holy and Righteous One, the Prince of life who was prophesied from ancient times to come, to suffer and to die for our sins. This leads us to repentance and brings forgiveness. We will have times of refreshing as we eagerly await the completion of the time of restoration of sinners and Jesus' return to earth. We rejoice that God turns us from our sins.

Result: All the families of the earth will be blessed.

<u>Ask yourself</u>: Why would I be counted among those who are blessed since I am not of the descendants of Abraham?

Who are the descendants of Abraham and what do I need to be counted among the blessed?

Day 14 ~ Belief in God's Faithfulness

Read 1 John 1:5-10

1 John 1:9 *"If we confess our sins, God is faithful and righteous (just) to forgive us our sins and to cleanse us from all unrighteousness."*

Goal: Belief in God's faithfulness to forgive sin

Obstacles: Darkness, lying, denial of sin, and deceiving oneself

Affirmations: John's message is that God is light and in Him there is no darkness at all, and that if we walk in God's light, we have fellowship with other believers and are cleansed from sin by the blood of Jesus. If we confess our sins, God is faithful and righteous to forgive us our sins and to cleanse us from all unrighteousness since it was Jesus – the Savior of the world – who died to pay our sin debt.

Personal Application of the Precepts: As believers, we are not uninformed of the message declared by Jesus that God is light, and if we walk in God's light, we have fellowship with other believers and are cleansed from all our sins by the blood of Jesus. We know that if we confess our sins, God is faithful and righteous to forgive us our sins and to cleanse us from all unrighteousness. We can trust that Jesus died to pay our entire sin debt.

Result: We believe that God is faithful to forgive us our sins and to cleanse us from all unrighteousness.

Ask yourself: How can I be sure God has forgiven me all my sins – even those sins that seem unforgivable?

How can I be encouraged if I still feel guilt and shame even after confessing my sin to God?

Day 15 ~ Be Found Blameless

Read 1 Corinthians 1:4-9

1 Cor. 1:8 *"...who shall also confirm you to the end, blameless in the day of our Lord Jesus Christ."*

Goal: To be found blameless

Obstacles: Unrighteousness, and unbelief

Affirmations: Paul writes that the grace of God is given you in Christ Jesus, that you are enriched in Him, and the testimony of Christ is confirmed in believers. Believers are not lacking in any gift and are awaiting the revelation of Jesus Christ. He will confirm you to the end, blameless. God is faithful and has called you into fellowship with His Son Jesus Christ.

Personal Application of the Precepts: God's grace is given to believers in Christ Jesus, and we are enriched in Him. Believers are confirmed by the testimony of Christ Jesus and we are not lacking in any spiritual gift/ability which God gives us in order that we may serve Him. We eagerly wait for the appearing of our Lord Jesus Christ who shall also confirm us blameless. God called us into fellowship with His Son.

Result: Believers know the faithfulness of God to authenticate us blameless in Christ Jesus.

Ask yourself: Why do I firmly believe that God is faithful to validate me blameless in Christ Jesus?

What do I have to do to be declared blameless?

Day 16 ~ Promise for a Future

Read Jeremiah 29:8-14

Jer. 29:11 *"'For I know the plans that I have for you,' declares the Lord, 'plans for welfare and not for calamity to give you a future and a hope.'"*

Goal: To receive God's promise for a future

Obstacles: Being deceived by false prophets, searching for truth in wrong places, and sin

Affirmations: In his letter, Jeremiah warns his readers, "Do not listen to dreamers who teach false doctrine." Jeremiah declares the words of the Lord, "I know the plans I have for you, plans to give you a future and a hope." Jeremiah says that God will listen to your prayers, that if you will seek Him, you will find Him when you search for Him with all your heart, and that He will restore you.

Personal Application of the Precepts: We are warned not to listen to false preachers and teachers, but rather to seek the Lord and to search for Him with all our hearts and He will be found. We can trust in the Lord's promise that He has a plan for us

– to give us a future and not calamity. We are promised that God will listen to believers' prayers.

Result: We have God's promise for a future.

Ask yourself: How am I trusting in God's promise for a future for me or am I anxious for what the future holds for me?

How do I discern false teaching from truth?

Day 17 ~ Peace of Mind

Read Philippians 4:6-9

Phil. 4:7 *"And the peace of God, which surpasses all comprehension, shall guard your hearts and your minds in Christ Jesus."*

Goal: To have peace of mind

Obstacles: Anxiety, lies, wrongdoing, evil, sin, and prayerlessness

Affirmations: Paul says that the peace of God, which surpasses all understanding, will keep your hearts and your minds in Christ Jesus. Whatever is true, honorable, right, of good repute, of excellence and worthy of praise, to let your minds dwell on these things, to practice what is good and right, and the God of peace shall be with you.

Personal Application of the Precepts: We know that negative thinking and worry and anxiety cause stress, but we have been given the remedy to combat this. We are to let our minds dwell on whatever is true, whatever is worthy of respect, whatever is right, whatever is of good repute, whatever is of excellence, and whatever is worthy of praise. If we practice and get in the habit of pursuing what is good and what is right, we are promised that the God of peace will be with us and will keep our hearts and minds in Christ Jesus.

Result: We will have peace of mind.

Ask yourself: How can I have peace of mind and avoid my mind being in a constant state of anxiety?

How do I let my mind dwell on things that are true, right, and good?

Day 18 ~ Answered Prayer

Read John 14:1-14

John 14:13-14 *"And whatever you ask in My name, that I will do that the Father may be glorified in the Son. ¹⁴If you ask Me anything in My name, I will do it."*

Goal: To receive answered prayer

Obstacles: Troubled hearts, unbelief, rejection of Jesus, and asking outside of God's will

Affirmations: John relates how Jesus is preparing a place for you and will come to receive you. Jesus is the way, the truth, and the life, and no one comes to the Father except through Him. Jesus is in the Father and the Father is in Him, and all the works Jesus did points to truth of who He is to help us believe in Him. The works we do will point others to Jesus, and whatever we ask in Jesus' name that glorifies the Father, Jesus will do.

Personal Application of the Precepts: We need not have troubled hearts, but only believe in Jesus. We follow Jesus because we believe He is the way, the truth, and the life, and there is no one else, no other way, to eternal life except through Jesus. We believe that Jesus and the Father are one – we cannot accept one without the other. We see the works of Jesus and hear His teaching, and so we believe. We trust in the powerful and holy name of Jesus. We know that to pray in His name means praying for the same things which Jesus would desire to see accomplished.

Result: We know that whatever we pray for in Jesus' name that brings glory to the Father, we will receive it.

Ask yourself: How do I sync my desires to what Christ desires, so my prayers are answered?

How do I recognize answered prayer if God answers my prayer differently than what I asked?

Day 19 ~ Transgressions Wiped Out

Read Isaiah 43:22-27

Is. 43:25 *"I, even I, am the One who wipes out your transgressions for My own sake, and I will not remember your sins."* (ESV)

Goal: To know my transgressions are wiped out

Obstacles: Prayerlessness and sins

Affirmations: Isaiah says of the Lord that He has not burdened His people with offerings and sacrifices, but the people wearied Him with their iniquities. Yet He is the One who blots out their transgressions for His own sake, and that He will remember their sins no more. The Lord gives man opportunity to prove himself right only to discover that he is a product of the sinful human nature, and if left to himself, he would be destroyed because of his sin.

Personal Application of the Precepts: We can trust that the words applied to the people of Israel also apply to us in that we too, weary the Lord with our sins and lack of prayer. We can make excuses for our sins, blame others, minimize our sins' seriousness, or even deny our sins, but if the Lord would leave us in that state, we would be destroyed. However, the Lord promises to wipe away our sins for His own sake and will not remember them anymore since He could foresee Jesus' death on the cross for the forgiveness of sins.

Result: We know that God will remember our sins no more, because He has blotted out (wiped away) all our sins.

Ask yourself: How have I tried to justify my sins rather than to take ownership of them and confess them?

How can I encourage others to know that the Lord wipes out our sins for His own sake?

Day 20 ~ Let Love be Genuine

Read Romans 12:9-21

Rom. 12:9-10 *"Let love be genuine. Abhor what is evil, hold fast to what is good. ¹⁰Love one another with brotherly affection. Outdo one another in showing honor."* (ESV)

Goal: To learn how to let love be genuine

Obstacles: Jealousy, want of control, placing conditions on loving, hypocrisy, evil, selfishness, being haughty in mind, self-elevation over others, showing disrespect, being argumentative and being revengeful

Affirmations: Paul encourages his readers to let love be genuine without hypocrisy, to hate what is evil and to cling to that which is good, to honor and be devoted to one another, to serve the Lord fervently, to rejoice in hope and persevere in trials, to give to those in need and to show hospitality, to bless and curse not, to come alongside others in their sorrow and in their joy, to respect what is right, to take no revenge on others, and to overcome evil with good.

Personal Application of the Precepts: Believers receive a "how to" guide to let love be genuine without hypocrisy. If we hate what is evil and cling to that which is good, if we honor and are devoted to others, if we serve the Lord fervently, if we rejoice in hope and persevere in trials, if we give to the needy and show hospitality, if we learn to bless and curse not, if we share in another's sorrow and in their joy, if we take no revenge, and if we overcome evil with good, we will obtain the goal.

Result: We will let love be genuine without hypocrisy.

Ask yourself: How can I seek ways to let my love for others be genuine and not love conditionally?

If God loved me conditionally, what changes would I need to make to keep His love towards me genuine?

Day 21 ~ Assurance that God is God

Read Isaiah 46:8-11

Is. 46:9 *"Remember the former things long past, for I am God and there is no other, I am God and there is no one like Me..."*

Goal: To have the assurance that God is God

Obstacles: Forgetfulness of God, doubt, and unbelief

Affirmations: Isaiah records God's declaration that He is God when He says, "I am God and there is no one like Me." God declares the end from the beginning with 100% accuracy. He is sovereign in that He will establish His purpose and He will do it. He will accomplish all for His good pleasure. He has spoken and will bring it to pass. He planned it and He will do it.

Personal Application of the Precepts: We, as believers, can be encouraged that our God is the true and sovereign God from all that is written from ages past and that there is no other god. We see His word declared and fulfilled with complete accuracy and since His purpose is established, we can trust He will do it. We believe that His good pleasure is for our good, His glory, and therefore, He will bring it to fruition. We trust that whatever He has planned, He will do.

Result: We are assured and encouraged when we believe that God is God, and there is no other.

Ask yourself: Knowing and believing this truth, how does this affect how I pray?

How can I encourage others to be assured of the one true God?

Day 22 ~ Wait with Eager Expectation

Read John 14:1-14

John 14:3 "*And if I go to prepare a place for you, I will come again, and receive you to myself, that where I am, there you may be also.*"

Goal: To wait with eager expectation

Obstacles: Impatience, doubt, unbelief

Affirmations: John lists specific encouragements to his readers from Jesus such as: provision in the Father's house ("In My Father's house are many dwelling places"), the promise to return ("And if I go to prepare a place for you, I will come again, and receive you to Myself…"), the prospect of doing greater works than He did ("Truly, truly, I say to you, he who believes in Me, the works that I do shall he do also, and greater works than these shall he do."), and the promise of answered prayer ("If you ask Me anything in My name, I will do it").

Personal Application of the Precepts: Believers, whether Jew or Gentile, can be encouraged in the promises of Jesus that He is preparing a place for us in His Father's house. We trust that He will return to receive us to Himself as He has said He would. We are encouraged to know that we have the potential of doing greater works through the power of the Holy Spirit, and we have the promise of answered prayer that if we ask anything that would honor God in Jesus name, He will do it.

Result: We can wait with eager expectation.

Ask yourself: How am I eagerly waiting for Christ's return and not get bogged down with worldly cares and concerns?

How do I redirect my actions from meaningless tasks to works that count for eternity?

Day 23 ~ Fullness of Joy & Pleasures Forevermore

Read Psalm 16

Ps. 16:11 *"You make known to me the path of life; in Your presence is fullness of joy; at Your right hand are pleasures forevermore."* (ESV)

Goal: To have fullness of joy and pleasures forevermore

Obstacles: Belief in false gods

Affirmations: David pours out his trust for the Lord to be his portion in life: "I take refuge in You, You are my Lord," the Lord is the portion of his inheritance and his heritage is beautiful to him. He sets the Lord continually before him and trusts Him for protection, for his joy, and for his security. He trusts the Lord in his death that he will not be abandoned in the grave but will be raised up to fullness of joy in the presence of the Lord with pleasures forevermore.

Personal Application of the Precepts: We too can trust in the Lord to be a refuge for us. We also can know that the Lord is our inheritance and that our heritage is beautiful. We can rest assured that the Lord will protect us, that we have joy and security. Even in death, we need not fear abandonment, but rather we will be raised up to dwell in the presence of the Lord forever.

Result: We will know the fullness of joy and the pleasures of the Lord forevermore.

Ask yourself: What does fullness of joy mean to me?

What pleasures at the right hand of the Lord do I take special delight in? Worship? Discovery of more of God? Praise? Serving the Lord? Listening to the Lord? Rejoicing? We can only imagine.

Day 24 ~ True Wisdom

Read 1 Corinthians 2:2-13

1 Cor. 2:7 *"These things we also speak, not in words which man's wisdom teaches but which the Holy Spirit teaches, comparing spiritual things with spiritual."*

Goal: To know true wisdom

Obstacles: Belief in clever arguments of men, misplaced faith, and unbelief

Affirmations: Paul's letter to the Corinthians describes the futility of man's wisdom compared to the superiority of God's wisdom. True wisdom is demonstrated in the power of the Holy Spirit, and God's wisdom is a mystery, the hidden wisdom, which God predestined before the ages for our glory – namely, Jesus Christ as Savior. God's wisdom cannot be understood by man unless the Spirit of God reveals it to him, and God gave us the Spirit that we might know and understand the things freely given to us by God.

Personal Application of the Precepts: We are enlightened by God's wisdom when we believe in Jesus Christ, and therefore, we see the foolishness and the meaninglessness of worldly wisdom. We receive the hidden mystery that was predestined before the ages, that by faith through the power of the Holy Spirit we might know and understand the things of God which He freely gives to those who believe.

Result: We have true wisdom.

Ask yourself: How can I gain true wisdom from God and not trust in the wisdom and traditions of man?

What is my greatest obstacle against receiving true wisdom from God?

Day 25 ~ Assurance of Eternal Life

Read John 5:19-25

John 5:24 *"Truly, truly, I say to you, he who hears My word, and believes Him who sent Me, has eternal life, and does not come into judgment, but has passed out of death into life."*

Goal: To have the assurance of eternal life

Obstacles: Unbelief, sin, and denying the Father and the Son

Affirmations: John emphasizes the words of Jesus that the Father and the Son are one. The Father shows all things to the Son. Just as the Father raises the dead and gives them life, even so the Son gives life. The Father gives all authority to Jesus to judge the unrighteous, and whoever hears the words of Jesus and believes has eternal life, and does not come into judgment, but has passed out of death into life. All believers who have previously died shall also hear Jesus' voice and be raised up.

Personal Application of the Precepts: We can be encouraged to know that the Father and the Son are one, and that just as the Father raises the dead, even so, Jesus will raise believers from the dead and give life. We can be confident that when Jesus judges the unrighteous, we do not have to fear because Jesus has said that whoever hears His words and believes shall have eternal life and does not come into judgment. We trust that the believers who have died before us will also hear Jesus' voice and will be raised up to eternal life.

Result: We have the assurance of eternal life.

Ask yourself: How do I squelch doubts that I have received eternal life?

How do I encourage others to believe in Jesus in order that they may have eternal life?

Day 26 ~ Clear Conscience

Read Hebrews 10:19-27

Heb. 10:22 *"...let us draw near with a sincere heart in full assurance of faith, having our hearts sprinkled clean from an evil conscience and our bodies washed with pure water..."*

Goal: To have a clear conscience

Obstacles: Rejection of Jesus, rejection of God's truths, unforgiven sin, wavering in weak faith, doubt, and willful sin

Affirmations: The author of Hebrews testifies that Christ died for our sins, and He is our great high priest. Therefore, we can draw near with a sincere heart in full assurance of faith, having our hearts sprinkled clean from all sin, we can hold fast the confession of our hope for He who promised it is faithful, we should stimulate and encourage each other to love and good works, and if we go on sinning willfully after receiving the knowledge of the truth, there is no other sacrifice for sin available and no other way to come to God – only judgment remains.

Personal Application of the Precepts: Believers can trust that Christ died for our sins, the Righteous for the unrighteous, and that He is our great high priest. Therefore, we can approach the throne of God with a sincere heart with full assurance of faith in the confession of our hope because Jesus who promised this is faithful and true. We are encouraged when we meet together to stimulate each other to love and good works.

Result: We have a clear conscience.

Ask yourself: How can I keep a clear conscience?

How do I encourage others to love and good works?

Day 27 ~ Renewal

Read 2 Corinthians 4:8-16

2 Cor. 4:16 *"Therefore we do not lose heart, but though our outer man is decaying, yet our inner man is being renewed day by day."*

Goal: To be renewed

Obstacles: Affliction, being perplexed, persecution, and man's mortality

Affirmations: Paul reminds his readers that believers are not crushed, not despairing, not forsaken, and not destroyed, that the life of Jesus is manifested in mortal flesh, that we have the spirit of faith knowing that God will raise us along with all believers and because of grace, we can give thanks to the glory of God, and we are encouraged to know that the inner man is being renewed.

Personal Application of the Precepts: We are encouraged to know that whatever affliction or trial we may encounter, we will not be destroyed. Our faith is made strong knowing that our heavenly Father will raise us up and because of His grace, we can give thanks to the glory of God.

Result: Our inner man is being renewed day by day.

Ask yourself: If I am discouraged easily, how can I rejoice more often that my inner self is being renewed?

Why does knowing that I will be raised up to eternal life give me cause to glorify God?

Day 28 ~ Wait for the Lord

Read Lamentations 3:21-33

Lam. 3:25 *"The Lord is good to those who wait for Him, to the person who seeks Him."*

Goal: To learn to wait for the Lord.

Obstacles: Impatience, unbelief, grumbling, sin, and defiance.

Affirmations: Jeremiah gives great hope when he writes that the Lord's loving kindness never ceases, His compassion never fails, His faithfulness is great, He is good to those who wait for Him, it is good for man to wait silently, to have total submission and complete surrender to the Lord, and the Lord does not afflict willingly.

Personal Application of the Precepts: Believers know and understand that the Lord does not afflict us willingly, but in order that we would have total submission and complete surrender to Him for our good. We have hope when we trust in the Lord's never-ending, loving kindness, His unfailing compassion, and His great faithfulness. We are encouraged to know that He is good to those who wait silently for Him; to be still and know He is God.

Result: We wait patiently for the Lord.

Ask yourself: If I grumble and complain about my unpleasant circumstances, how can I rather wait silently for the Lord?

What must I do to surrender completely, to totally submit to the Lord?

Day 29 ~ Deliverance from Darkness

Read Galatians 1:3-10

Gal. 1:4 *"...who gave Himself for our sins, that He might deliver us out of this present evil age, according to the will of our God and Father."*

Goal: To have deliverance from darkness

Obstacles: Sin, unbelief, belief in false teachings, and departure from grace to retreat into law

Affirmations: In his letter to the Galatians, Paul encourages believers that since Jesus gave Himself for our sins, He would deliver us out of the present darkness according to the will of the Father. There is no other gospel but the gospel of the grace of Christ, and anyone who preaches otherwise should be accursed. The cross-centered way cannot be viewed as seeking to please men but is of God.

Personal Application of the Precepts: Believers can be fully assured that since Jesus gave Himself for our sins, He will deliver us out of this present darkness according to the will of the Father. Since we belong to God, believers have the discernment to judge between the gospel of the grace of Christ and any other gospel that is of man. We can be confident that the cross-centered gospel is of God.

Result: We are delivered from darkness.

<u>Ask yourself:</u> How can I be certain that once delivered from darkness I am always delivered?

How do I refute other teachings from the gospel of Christ so that I would not be deceived?

Day 30 ~ Live in the Moment

Read Luke 12:16-28

Luke 12:25 *"And which of you by being anxious can add a single hour to his span of life?"* (ESV)

Goal: To live in the moment

Obstacles: Worry and anxiety, planning with no regard for the present, materialism, lack of trust, and lack of faith.

Affirmations: Luke records Jesus' own words that it is foolish to plan, to build, and to work for earthly future security at the expense of neglecting the treasures of living in the present and enjoying a relationship with Him. God feeds the birds, and we are of more value, so why do we worry? If God so clothes the lilies of the filed, He will certainly provide for His children.

Personal Application of the Precepts: Believers in Christ need not worry over temporary needs knowing that God will provide our necessities of food and clothing. We are invited to consider that since He provides for the birds and cares for the flowers, He will certainly do this and more for us.

We can trust Him in all things and turn our focus on Him at all times.

Result: We will live in the moment and need not worry about the mundane.

Ask yourself: How would my life be different if I were not anxious or if I did not worry?

How do I overcome anxiety, worry, and fear?

Day 31 ~ Abundant Life

Read John 10:7-15

John 10:10 *"The thief comes only to steal, and kill, and destroy. I came that they might have life and might have it abundantly."*

Goal: To have abundant life

Obstacles: False teachers, the thief who comes to steal, kill, and destroy, and prosperity preachers

Affirmations: John quotes the words of Jesus when He says, "Truly, truly, I say to you, I am the door of the sheep. If anyone enters through Me, he shall be saved." And again, He says, "I came that they (believers) might have life and might have it abundantly." John reiterates that Jesus, as the Good Shepherd, lays down His life for the sheep, knows His own, and they know Him.

Personal Application of the Precepts: Believers trust in Jesus and are assured that because Jesus laid down His life for us, we are known to Him, and we shall be saved for eternity. We are given abundant life. We are strengthened to know that Jesus, as the Good Shepherd, protects us and cares for us.

Result: We can know and enjoy abundant life on earth.

Ask yourself: How would I explain abundant life and am I really enjoying abundant life? Why or why not?

What is my defense against the thief who comes to steal, kill, and destroy?

Day 32 ~ Spirit-filled

Read John 16:7-15

John 16:7 *"But I tell you the truth, it is to your advantage that I go away, for if I do not go away, the Helper shall not come to you, but if I go, I will send Him to you."*

Goal: To be Spirit-filled

Obstacles: Sin and unbelief

Affirmations: John records the words of Jesus concerning the Holy Spirit: "I will send Him to you." The Holy Spirit convicts the world of sin of which the greatest and most basic one is unbelief. The Holy Spirit also convicts believers of sin that we must confess. Concerning righteousness: the Holy Spirit convinces people of the truthfulness of the gospel, so we are enabled to believe. Concerning judgment: the Holy Spirit reveals that at the cross, Christ triumphed over Satan serving notice to unbelievers of their judgment to come. The Holy Spirit guides us to all truth with all that He hears from Jesus and discloses to us what is to come.

Personal Application of the Precepts: Believers honor the work of the Holy Spirit because He was sent by Jesus to convict the world of sin and unbelief and to convict us of our sins that we may confess them. Through the Holy Spirit we are convinced of the truthfulness of the Gospel and the coming judgments on unbelievers. Therefore, we are made alive in our faith.

Result: We seek to be Spirit-filled. We are not to grieve nor quench the Spirit, but to yield to Him in all things.

<u>Ask yourself</u>: What does it mean to me to be Spirit filled?

In what ways do I quench or grieve the Holy Spirit?

Day 33 ~ Hope in God

Read Psalm 42:6-11

Ps. 42:11 *"Why are you in despair, O my soul? And why have you become disturbed within me? Hope in God, for I shall yet praise Him, the help of my countenance, and my God."*

Goal: To have hope in God

Obstacles: Waves of sorrow that overwhelm, depression, despair, oppression, and inner turmoil

Affirmations: The writer, in the depths of distress, offers praise as the prescription for depression praying that the Lord will command His lovingkindness in the daytime, and His song in the night. God is a shelter amidst our enemies and hope in God is a surety for the help that comes from God.

Personal Application of the Precepts: Those of us who walk with God are encouraged to know that even in the throes of depression, despair, and distress, God has not abandoned us, but will deliver us. Believers learn that to praise God in even the severest of trials is the remedy for overcoming depression, despair, and inner turmoil.

Result: We have hope in God.

Ask yourself: Where do I put my hope in times of trial, despair, distress, and depression?

How do I look for the Lord's loving-kindness, for His song in the night when there is darkness all around?

Day 34 ~ Quiet and Gentle Spirit

Read 1 Peter 3:1-6

1 Peter 3:4 *"...but let it be the hidden person of the heart, with the imperishable quality of a gentle and quiet spirit, which is precious in the sight of God."*

Goal: To have a quiet and gentle spirit

Obstacles: Controlling spirit, disrespect, impurity, overly concerned with outward appearances, fear, and being boisterous

Affirmations: Peter gives tender encouragement to women/wives to be gentle and quiet in spirit that an unbelieving husband may be won without a word by a woman's quiet behavior which is precious to God. Sarah, who hoped in God, obeyed Abraham, and we have become children if we do what is right without giving in to fear.

Personal Application of the Precepts: As Christian women/wives, we can be encouraged and even be free from fear, to know that our quiet spirit, which is precious in God's sight, will do more towards winning husbands than harsh and disrespectful words could ever do. We need not fear

– only be still before the Lord and let our behavior speak the condition of our hearts.

Result: We will strive to have a quiet and gentle spirit.

Ask yourself: How do I become a woman with a quiet and gentle spirit when I am by nature a take-charge type of person?

Why do I feel the need to be in charge of situations and people, and how do I relinquish it?

Day 35 ~ Security

Read Isaiah 26:1-6

Is. 26:3 *"The steadfast of mind You will keep in perfect peace, because he trusts in You."*

Goal: To have security

Obstacles: Unrighteousness, unfaithfulness, doubt, lack of trust in the Lord, and wickedness

Affirmations: Isaiah writes of the day (millennium) when a song of rejoicing will be sung in Israel, because they will have a strong city, gates are opened for the faithful, and there is perfect peace for those whose mind is stayed on the Lord. God is the everlasting Rock to believers, but will judge the wicked righteously, and the afflicted will triumph.

Personal Application of the Precepts: Believers will sing and shout for joy when the land of Israel is redeemed. Those whose minds are stayed on the Lord, will have perfect peace and security in our God, the everlasting Rock, when He brings to pass our complete salvation and the judgment of the wicked. We will be brought out of our affliction into the triumph in the Lord.

Result: We will have security and perfect peace forevermore.

Ask Yourself: What is the root cause of my insecurity and anxiety, and how do I let go and let God be my rock?

How can I trust in the Lord, keep my mind on Him, and take to heart His encouragement to everlasting peace?

Day 36 ~ Strengthened with Power

Read Ephesians 3:6-19

Eph. 3:16 *"...that He would grant you, according to the riches of His glory, to be strengthened with power through His Spirit in the inner man."*

Goal: To be strengthened with power

Obstacles: Unbelief

Affirmations: Paul explains the mystery past that Gentiles are now included as fellow heirs, fellow members of the body, and fellow partakers of the promise of the Gospel in Christ Jesus. The manifold wisdom of God may be made known through the church according to the eternal purpose carried out in Christ Jesus. We have confident access to the throne of God through faith in Him. Paul's prayer would be answered for his readers to be strengthened with power through the Holy Spirit in the inner man, that Christ may dwell within our hearts through faith, and that we would comprehend and know the love of Christ.

Personal Application of the Precepts: Believers are encouraged to know that the gospel of salvation through faith in Jesus Christ is extended to all peoples as well as to the Jews. We are included as fellow heirs, fellow members of the body, and fellow partakers of the promise of the gospel, that is eternal life. We are considered the church through whom the manifold wisdom of God is revealed.

Result: We are strengthened with power through the indwelling Holy Spirit.

<u>Ask yourself</u>: How can I approach the throne of God with confidence?

How am I strengthened with power?

Day 37 ~ Peace with God

Read Romans 4:25-5:11

Rom. 5:1 *"Therefore having been justified by faith, we have peace with God through our Lord Jesus Christ."*

Goal: To have peace with God

Obstacles: No justification, no faith, sin, and an enemy of God

Affirmations: Paul writes that Jesus was delivered up because of our transgressions and was raised for our justification, so that by faith we have peace. We stand in grace through faith and exult in the hope of the glory of God, We are encouraged to exult in our tribulations which bring about perseverance, and perseverance leads to proven character, and proven character gives way to hope. The love of God has been poured out to us through the Holy Spirit. Christ died for us while we were yet sinners, and we are justified by His blood and shall be saved from the wrath of God. We are reconciled to God.

Personal Application of the Precepts: Believers can trust Jesus who was delivered up because of our sins and was raised for our justification. We stand in God's grace through faith and can exult in the hope of the glory of God. The love of God has been poured out within our hearts through the Holy Spirit. We are justified by His blood, and because we are reconciled to God, we shall be saved from the wrath of God.

Result: We have peace with God.

<u>Ask yourself</u>: On what am I basing my reconciliation with God?

How can I thank God for being reconciled to Him?

Day 38 ~ Exult in the Lord

Read Habakkuk 3:17-19

Hab. 3:18 *"Yet I will exult in the Lord, I will rejoice in the God of my salvation."*

Goal: To exult in the Lord

Obstacles: Dismayed at surrounding troubles, losing focus when attacked by the enemy, and fear amidst natural disasters

Affirmations: Habakkuk affirms his faith in the sovereign God even amidst an invasion of the enemy that strips the land bare. The fig tree does not blossom, no fruit on the vines, failed olive crop, bare fields, no flocks or cattle, and yet, he will exult in the Lord. He will rejoice in the sovereign God because the Lord is his strength, and God makes his footing sure like a hind's (gazelle) feet.

Personal Application of the Precepts: Believers can learn from Habakkuk that when trouble surrounds us, we can trust in the sovereign God to protect and deliver us. Our faith is strengthened when we rejoice and exult in God amidst calamity because we know that the Lord is our strength, and He makes our footing sure.

Result: We will exult in the Lord.

Ask yourself: What is my response amidst trials, and troubles, and turbulent times?

How do I get to the point of exulting in the Lord amidst the greatest of troubles?

Day 39 ~ Let us be Thankful

Read Hebrews 12:25-29

Heb. 12:28 *"Therefore, since we receive a kingdom which cannot be shaken, let us show gratitude, by which we may offer to God an acceptable service with reverence and awe..."*

Goal: To be thankful

Obstacles: Refusing to listen to those on earth who warn against sin and unbelief, turning away from Him who warns from heaven, and dying in unbelief

Affirmations: The author records the words of God, "Yet once more I will shake not only the earth, but also the heaven." The expression "Yet once more" denotes the removing of those created things in order that those things which cannot be shaken (the eternal kingdom) may remain. Believers will receive such an unshakeable kingdom. God is a consuming fire and will destroy all sin and evil.

Personal Application of the Precepts: Christians believe that the present heavens and earth will be destroyed because of sin, and God will make a new heaven and a new earth. This eternal kingdom cannot be shaken, and all believers belong to this eternal kingdom. Therefore, we are encouraged.

Result: We can be thankful.

Ask yourself: How can I show gratitude to God as an acceptable service with reverence and awe?

What does it mean to me that "God is a consuming fire?"

Day 40 ~ Rest for the Soul

Read Matthew 11:25-30

Matt. 11:28 *"Come to Me, all who are weary and heavy-laden, and I will give you rest.*

Goal: To find rest for the soul.

Obstacles: Heavy burdened, wise in own eyes, does not know God, unbelief, and trust in self.

Affirmations: Matthew states that God reveals truth to babes and not to those who are wise in their own eyes. The Son reveals the Father to whom He wills. Jesus invites all to come, receive salvation, and He beckons all to learn discipleship. He invites us to serve in yoke with the Lord, and that His yoke is easy compared to the teaching and requirements of man's religion.

Personal Applications of the Precepts: God reveals His truth to those who are not haughty or wise in their own eyes. Therefore, we put aside whatever wisdom we may have to gain the truths of God. Jesus extends an invitation to us to receive salvation, and He calls us to discipleship.

We are to be yoked with Him as He teaches us under His discipline because He cares for us and wants only the best for us. Jesus does not strap us with a heavy burden. Jesus' yoke is easy, and His burden is light, and we will find a better alternative to our futile striving.

Result: We will find rest for our souls.

Ask yourself: Why am I so weary and heavy-laden?

How does accepting Jesus' invitation to come to Him give me rest for my soul?

"The Lord is my portion," says my soul.
"Therefore I have hope in Him."

Lamentations 3:24

Dear Lord, I am strengthened and encouraged. Thank You for Your invitation to come to You that I may be uplifted, to find rest for my soul and peace in my heart!

Meet the Author

Rita Kroon was born in Minneapolis, but raised in St. Paul, MN.  She graduated from Sibley High School and received her associate's degree in speech / communications from Lakewood Community College.

She is an author, blogger, and Bible study group leader. She has written devotionals, Bible studies, novels, wildlife magazine articles, children's short stories, poetry, a humorous newspaper column "Rita Raps it up," and more.

Rita's current works are in memory of her husband, Burt, and their daughter, René. She has two other daughters, LaDawn and Shelly, and 17 grandchildren.

She lives in Lexington, MN.

Other Books by Rita Kroon

40 Days of Assurance is a daily devotional intended to give you assurance in your walk with God, or with your parenting skills, or with relationships, or with a lack of confidence with who you are as a person. Sometimes we just need loving arms around us, to be assured that everything will work out. Bring your empty cup to the Lord that He may fill it with your daily portion of His grace and discover the peace of God that surpasses all understanding that will keep your heart and mind in Christ Jesus.

ISBN: 9780989198530

40 Days in the Wilderness is a daily devotional booklet that gives insight to strengthen and to nourish you as you journey through your wilderness – a drought in your spiritual walk? A desert in your marriage with no oasis in sight? A dry spell at work or at school? Lacking peace? Take heart. Bring your empty cup to the Lord that He may fill it with your daily portion of His grace. Find the faith needed to sustain you. Be nourished and refreshed.

ISBN: 9780989198509

Cancer – a Journey through the Valley is  the story of one woman's journey through the valley whereupon she realized that her faith in God during the calm seasons of life necessitated a mighty strengthening if it was to sustain her on the battlefield. Discover how God worked such a faith. If you or a loved one is fighting cancer, be encouraged. You are not walking alone.

Know that the God who guides our steps
is the same God who directs our stops. Either way, he has us in the palm of His hand. Be amazed at His matchless grace.

ISBN: 9780989198516

Womanhood: Becoming a Woman of Virtue  is an interactive Bible study of eight inspirational women of the Old Testament and is suitable for individual or group setting. There are two parts: an in-depth section for the woman who likes to linger in the Word and a condensed segment for the woman on the go. The in depth section gives five weeks of study for each woman and can easily be structured to fit your time schedule. The condensed segment is an eight-week study with no homework.

Explore the lives of Eve, Sarah, Rebekah, Rachel, Miriam, Deborah, Tamar, and Esther who are ordinary women who find themselves in unprecedented circumstances. Be inspired by their faith, encouraged through their hardships, and challenged by their choices and decisions as you seek to become a woman of virtue.

ISBN: 9780989198554

Kiss Your Mommy Goodbye is a Christian novel. In his desperate quest to provide love and stability as a part-time father to young Maddy, Mike does the unthinkable. His actions got far more disastrous results than he could have ever imagined, and the very one he tried to protect would suffer the repercussions of his decision. In this riveting tale, a man struggles to reconcile and rebuild broken relationships and find peace with others and with God.

ISBN: 9780989198561

Letters from the Past is historical fiction. Eight women of the Bible write personal letters to today's woman. Each woman reveals the emotional impact that infertility, rape, incest, deception and betrayal, and family dysfunction had on her. In each of their stories, trial turns to triumph when the thread of God's faithfulness is traced through these women of ancient times to the women of the 21st century. Today's woman will be challenged and encouraged, find hope for the oppressed, and celebrate the accomplishments of Eve, Sarah, Rebekah, Rachel, Miriam, Deborah, Tamar, and Esther.

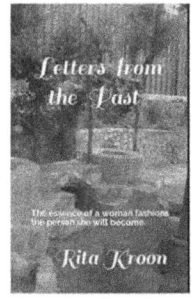

ISBN: 9780989198578

Praying the Scriptures is a collection of prayers  taken directly from Scripture since no word of God shall be void of power. When words cannot be found to say what is on your heart, this collection of prayers is meant to guide you during those times of solitude. Or, when words to express joy through praise and worship seem elusive, you can turn to the Scriptures. If praying is unfamiliar to you, or perhaps has long ago been abandoned, this book provides one way to begin afresh. Respond to the Lord's invitation to enter into a more intimate relationship with Him by praying His word.

ISBN: 9780989198585

Discover God through His Attributes is a
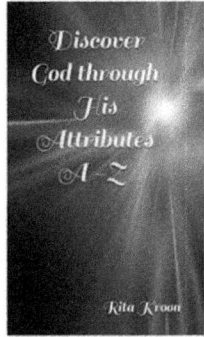
guide to help in the search for deeper and more meaningful relationship with God. Discover who He is. Be filled with awe. Give praise to the Lord of the heavens and the earth Reverence Him for who He is, for there is no other god or anything in the entire universe like Him. Give Him the honor due to His name. Be blessed as you discover God through His attributes and grow in your relationship with Him.

ISBN: 9780989198523

Nuggets from My Pocket is a collection of

tidbits of wisdom quotes, sayings, blessings, promises and more that have been gathered along the trail. These gems of truth will inspire and encourage you. They will give you cause to pause, time to wonder and ponder and a reason to reflect.

Nuggets from My Pocket is my gift to you for your pocket, or to share a nugget of encouragement with those around you.

Here's a nugget to ponder: "God gives evidence of His existence, but not proof since He always leaves room for faith."

ISBN: 9780989198592

More Nuggets from My Pocket is a collection of sayings, wit, insights, quotes, wisdom, promises, prayer, and more that were gathered where the trail led to an open meadow.

These gems will inspire you and encourage you no matter what path of life you travel. Stop to ponder the insights given, or to discover a fresh perspective, or to glean new meaning to old sayings.

More Nuggets from My Pocket is my way of giving you such an opportunity to explore rather than to merely hurry on your way. You may even want to share a nugget with a friend to encourage.

ISBN: 9798682187225

Extra Nuggets from My Pocket is a  collection of sayings meant to stir your imagination, fill your heart, and satisfy your desire for fresh "Ah, moments."

When the path of life leads me beside still waters, I search the beach for Extra Nuggets like one does when looking for agates on the North Shore. Some of these gems of truth, wit, quotes, prayers, blessings, and more are mine and some are those I gathered along the way and tucked into my pocket.

Come, walk with me along the beach and discover *Extra Nuggets from My Pocket* for your own pocket or to share with a friend.

ISBN: 9798587330566

Almost-Forgotten Nuggets is a collection of inspiring and wise sayings to capture your heart. This book is sure to take you on an adventure much like a treasure hunt where one seeks the next gem to keep for your pocket or to share with a friend along the way.

Here is a preview of what is inside – "Unconfessed sin is like a math problem: it divides the heart, adds woes, subtracts peace, and multiplies consequences."

Another peek – "It is sometimes difficult, but always good, to trust God with who you treasure most in this world."

ISBN: 9798511772042

John ~ A Mini Study is an interactive Bible study of the Gospel of John and is suitable for individual and group setting. It uses a loosely structured Observation, Interpretation, and Application method of study with summarizing Precepts in an easy-to-read format. One way to think of it like this: The *observation of facts* is like reading a menu. The *interpretation* is looking at the number of calories or the price on the menu. The *application questions* are the main course – the most satisfying part of the meal that energizes us for action. The *principle* is the appetizer that sharpens our desire for what is coming next. *Something to ponder* is the dessert and like most desserts, is just an occasional treat.

We learn what we can, apply what we know, and leave the rest to **God** is the *gratuity* we leave for the one who gave us dinner out ~ John, the disciple whom Jesus loved.

If we set a goal to connect with God and His truth every time we study His Word, we allow Him to mature us in our walk of faith.

"This is the disciple who testifies of these things and wrote these things, and we know this testimony is true." John 21:24   "BEHOLD! The Lamb of God!"

ISBN: 9798545633234

Pebbles of Truth is a collection of short, timeless sayings of truth that are filled with wisdom, give great insight, plus unforgettable quotes, thoughts, blessings, encouragement, blessings, and explore God's greatness. These pebbles of truth connect the heart with one's imagination much like pebbles on a beach connect the water and the land.

Here's a sneak peek: "Learn to write your hurts in the sand and to carve your blessings in stone." Here's another: "Man contributed nothing to his salvation except the sin that made it necessary."

Pebbles of Truth is sure to give you a delightful reading and sharing experience.

ISBN: 9798842917037

A Walk to the Well –

*A Place for Women to find Encouragement,
Hope, and Inspiration
through blogs, books, and Bible studies.*

www.awalktothewell.com

www.ingramcontent.com/pod-product-compliance
Lightning Source LLC
Chambersburg PA
CBHW071301040426
42444CB00009B/1815